# this letter tracingbook Belongs to

........................................

........................................

........................................

........................................

# LETTER TRACINGBOOK

# kids

# Write the Letter A

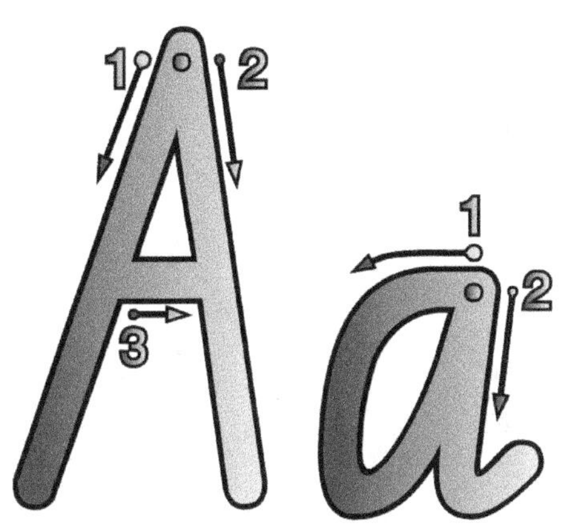

Aardvark

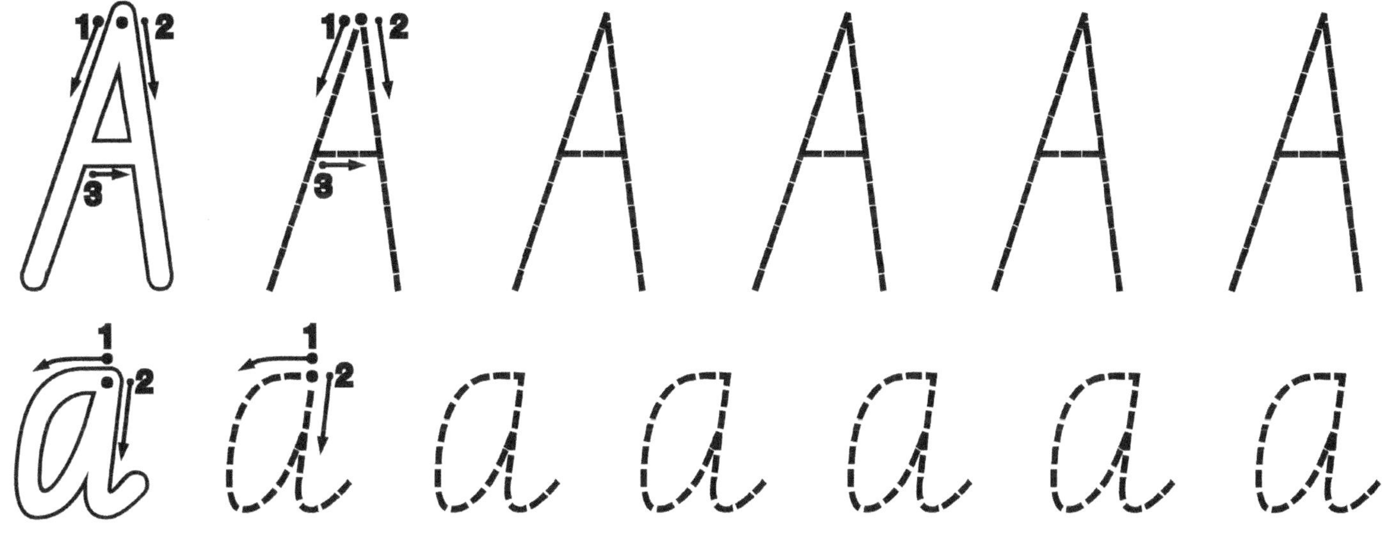

# Write the Letter B

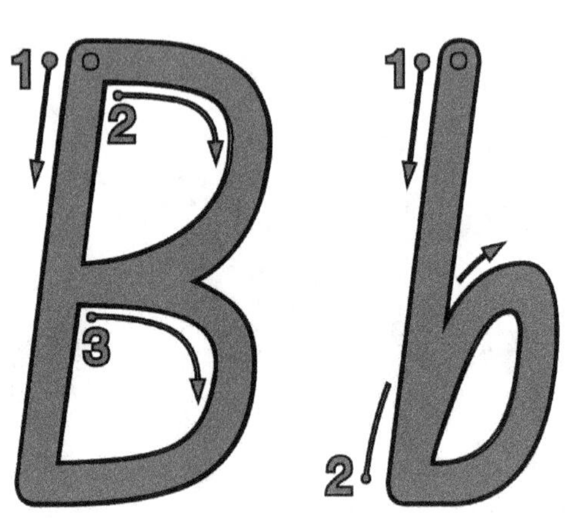

# Write the Letter c

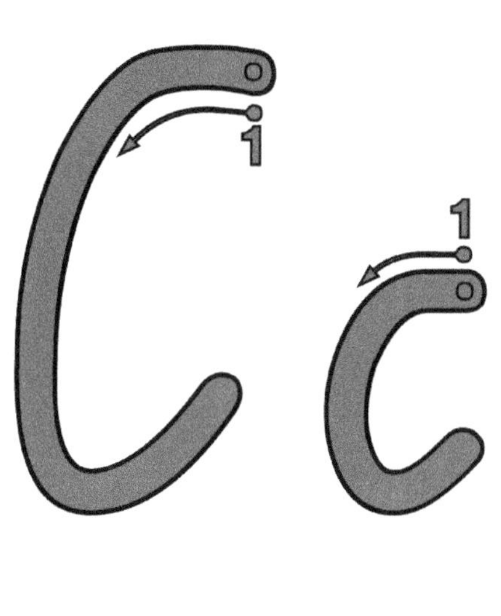

camel

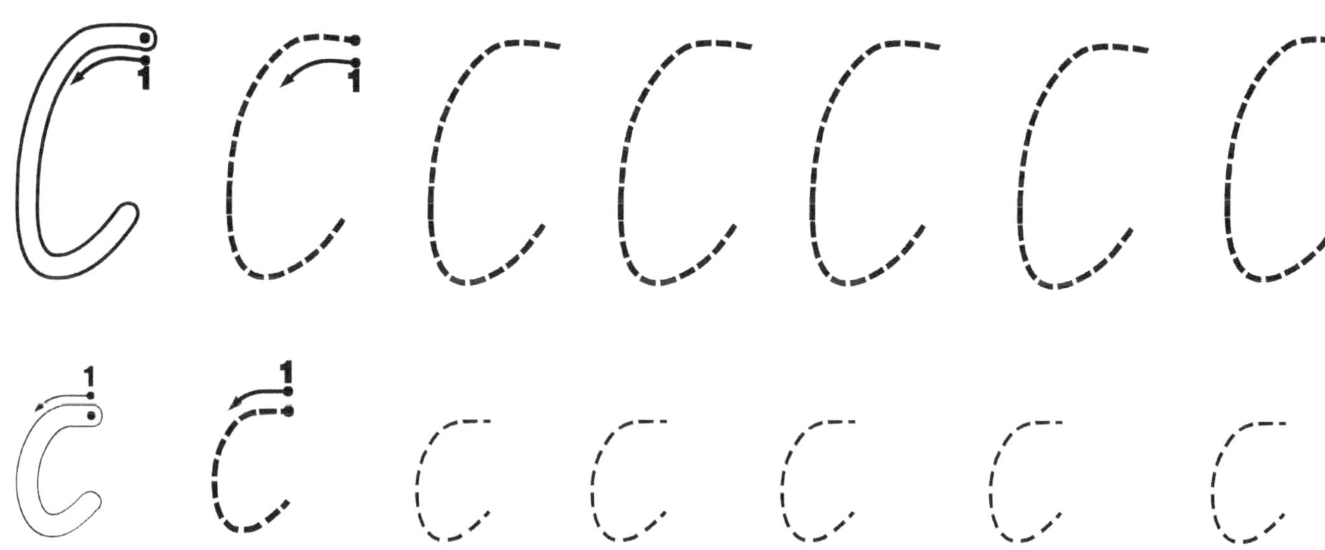

# Write the Letter D

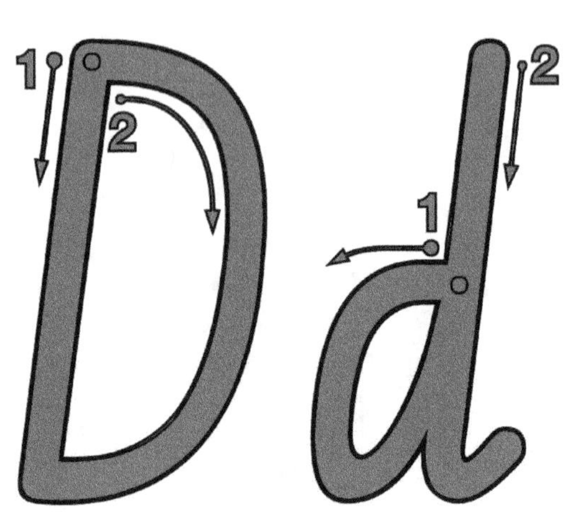

Dolphin

# Write the Letter E

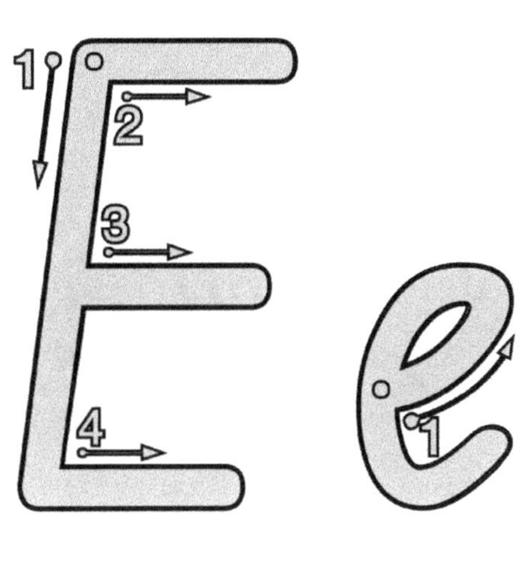

elephant

# Write the Letter F

# Write the Letter G

# Write the Letter H

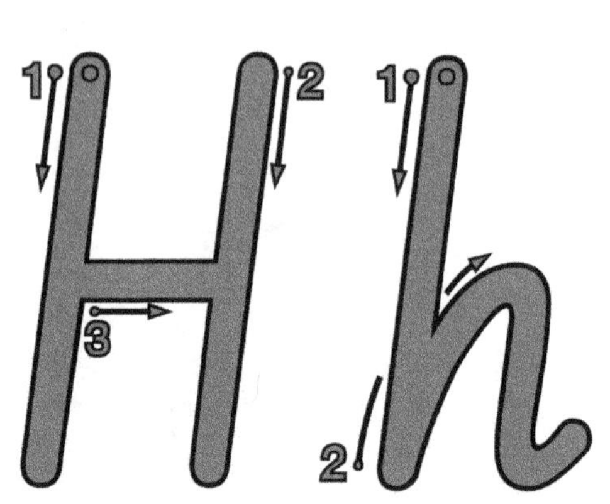

Horse

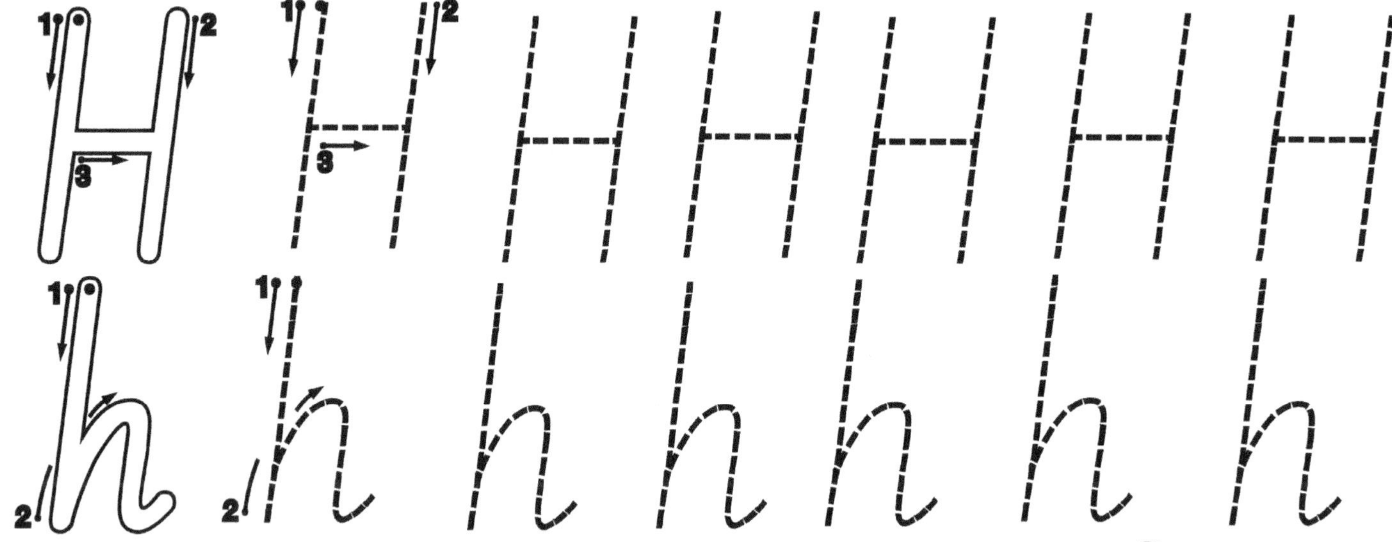

# Write the Letter I

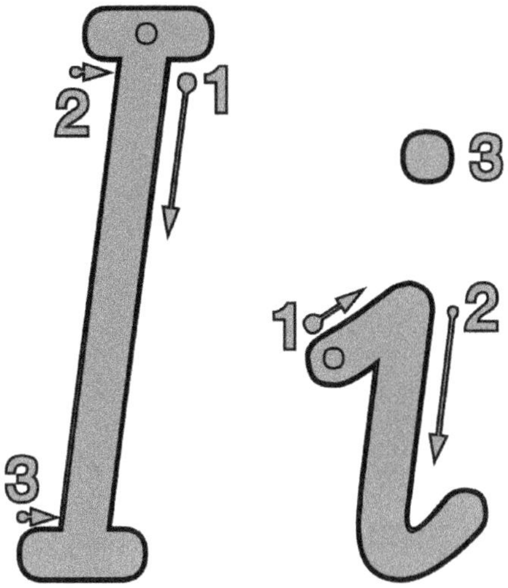

Impala

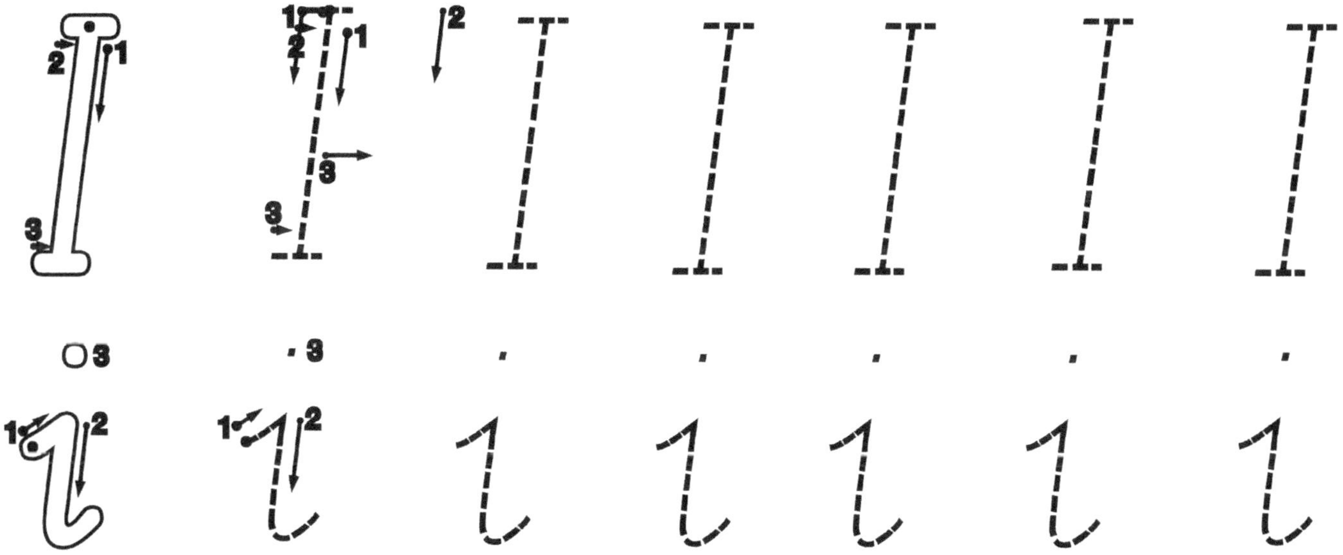

# Write the Letter J

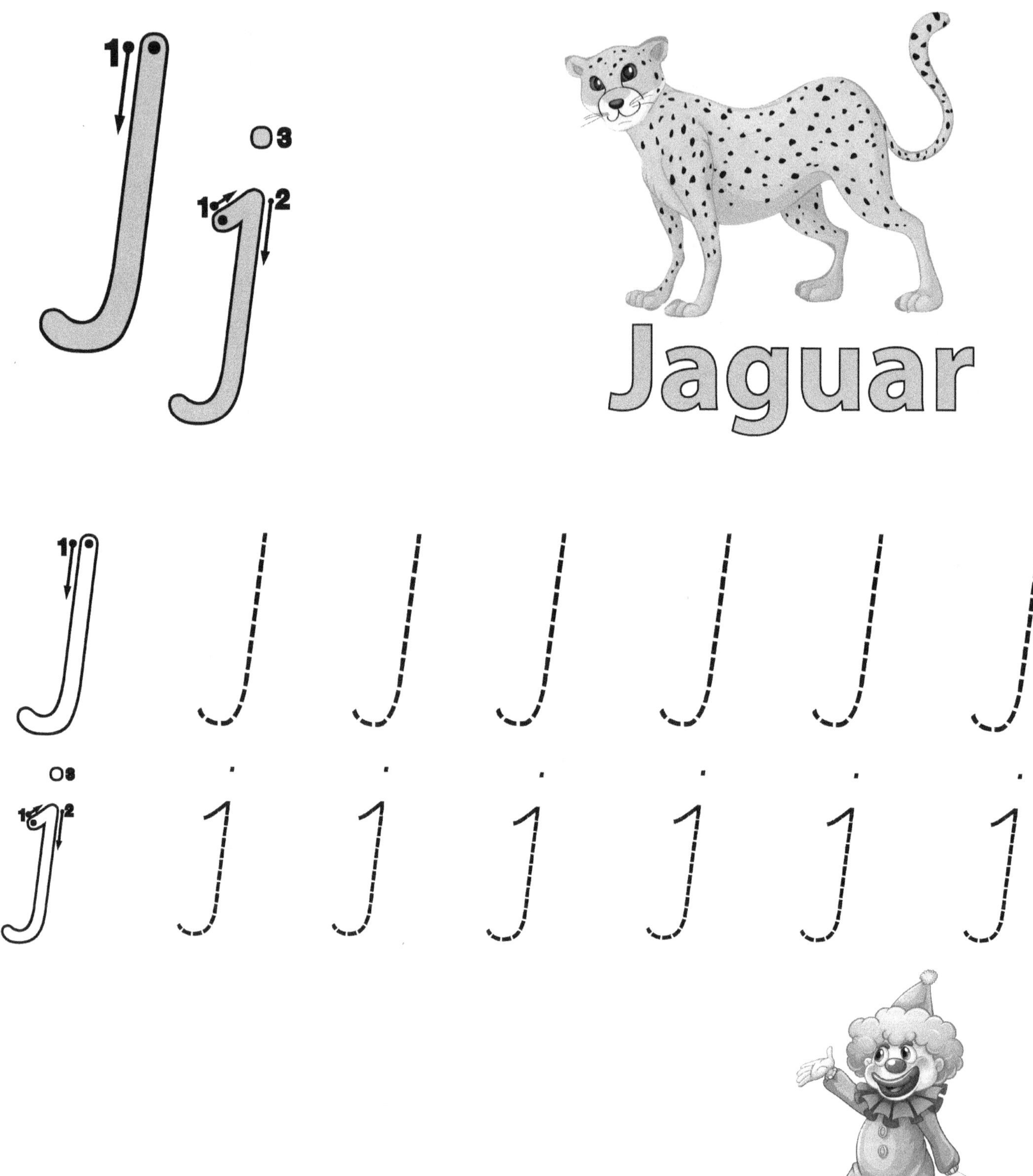

# Write the Letter K

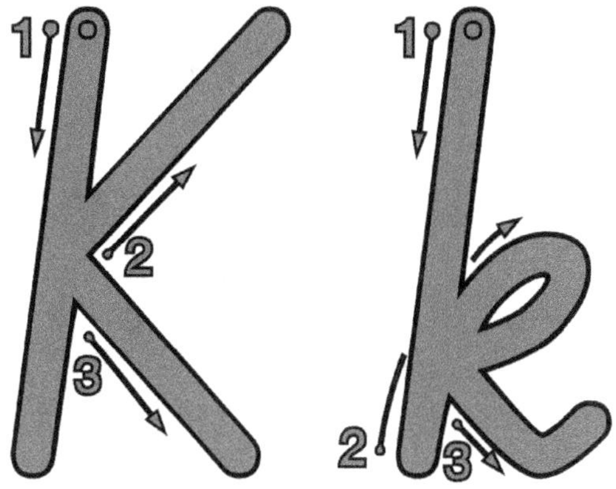

K k

Koala

# Write the Letter L

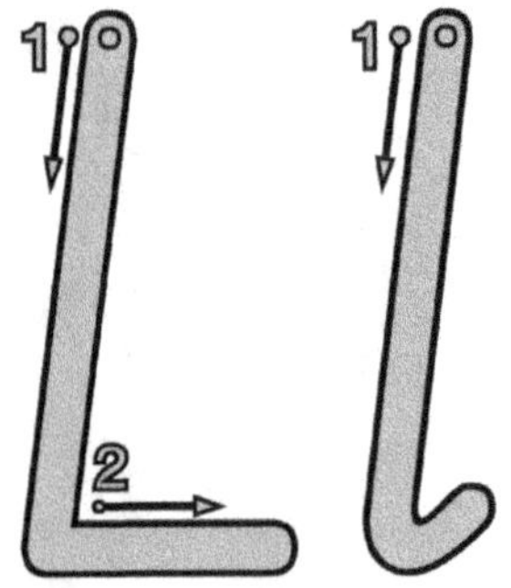

Ll

Lion

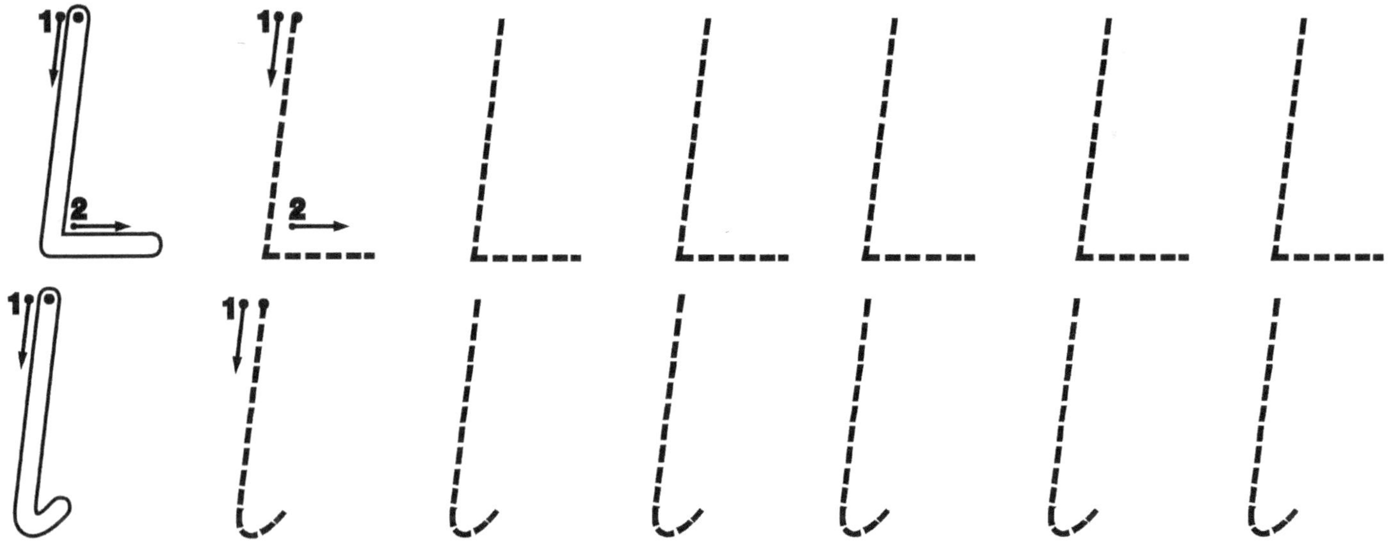

# Write the Letter M

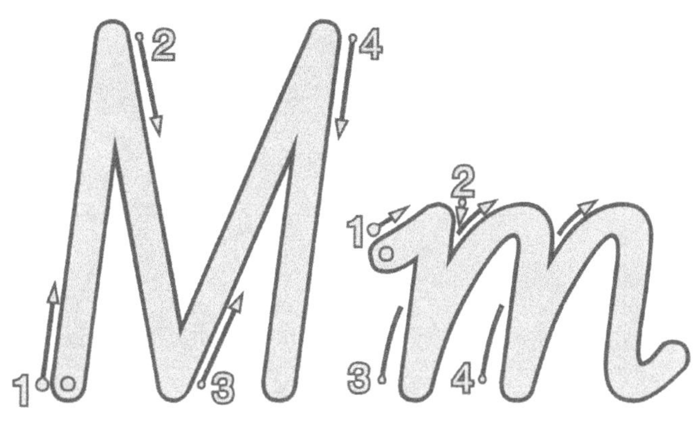

# Write the Letter N

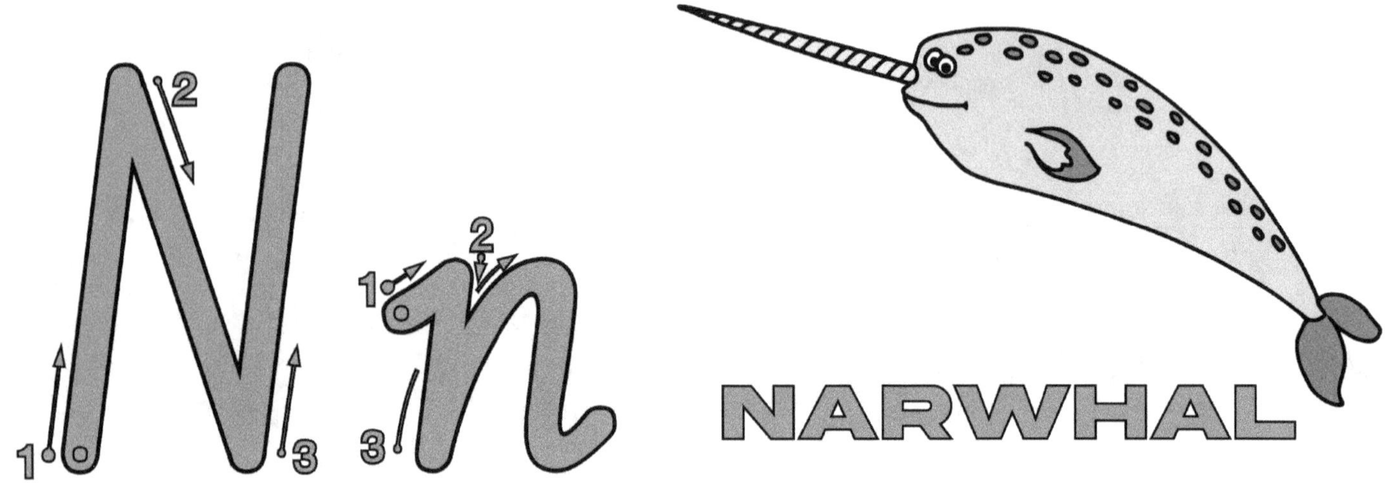

# Write the Letter O

# Write the Letter P

Parrot

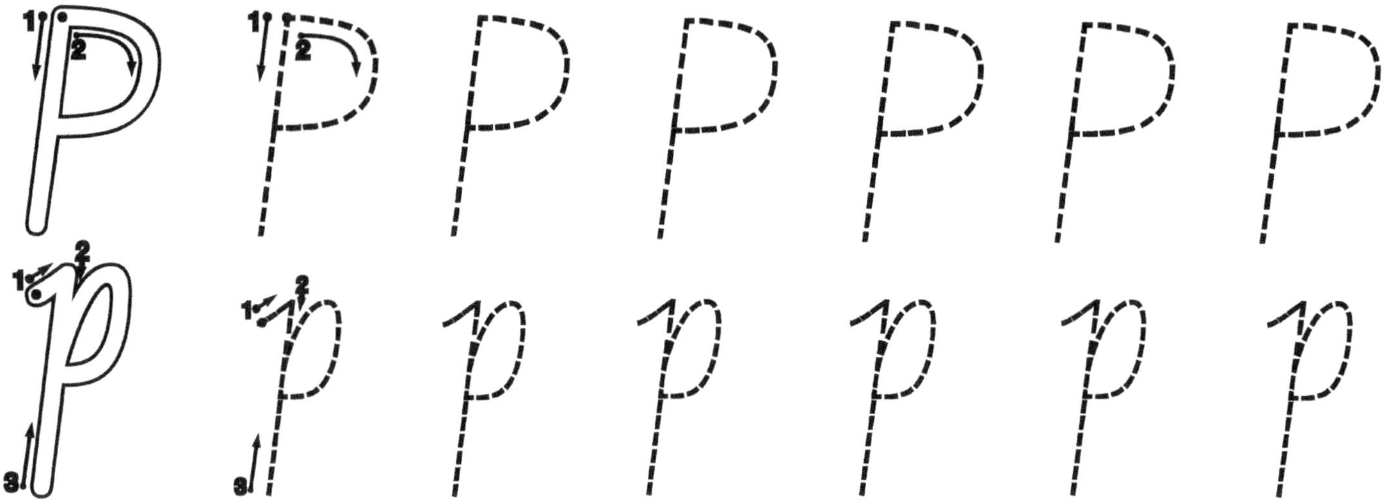

# Write the Letter Q

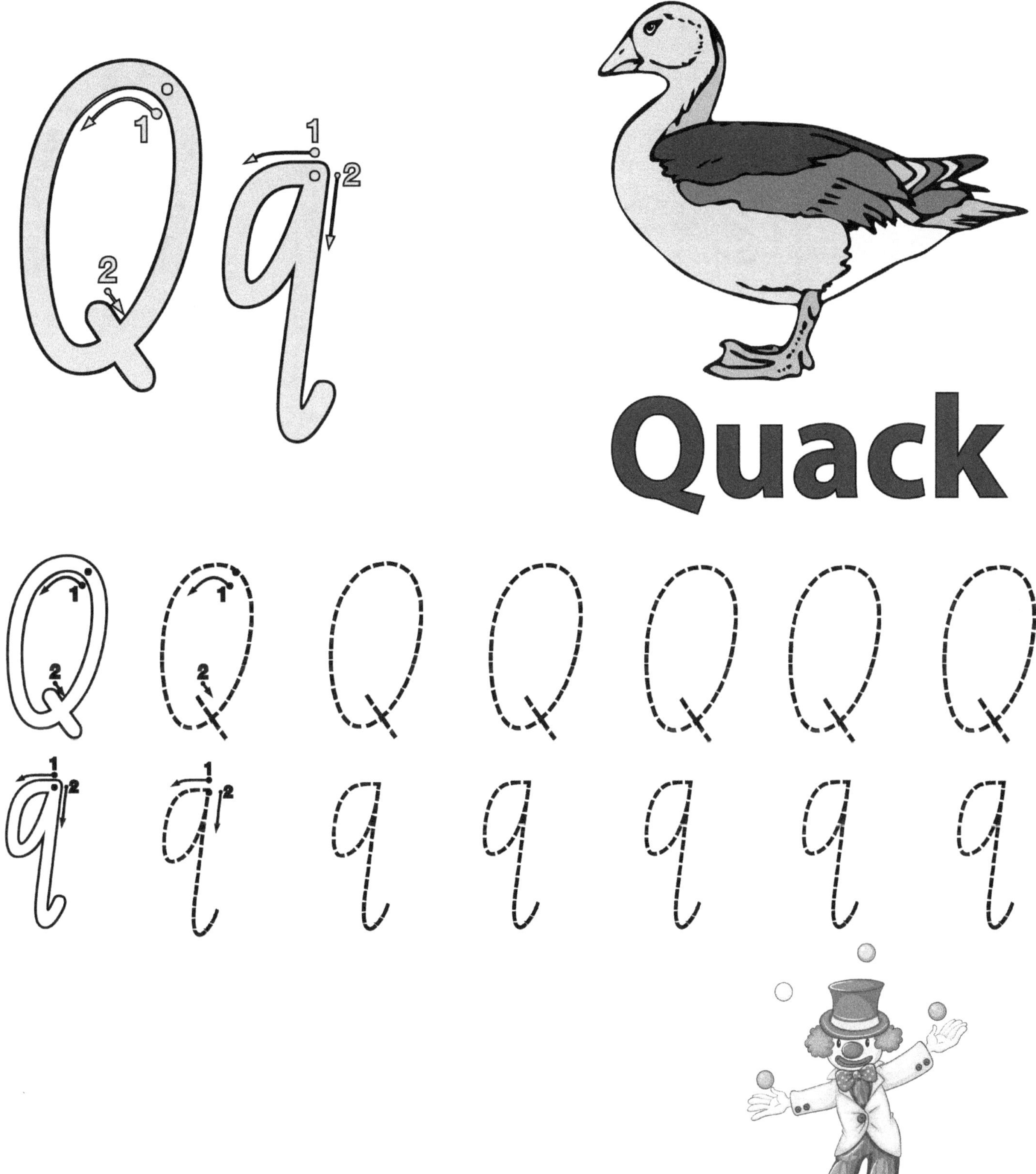

# Write the Letter R

# Write the Letter S

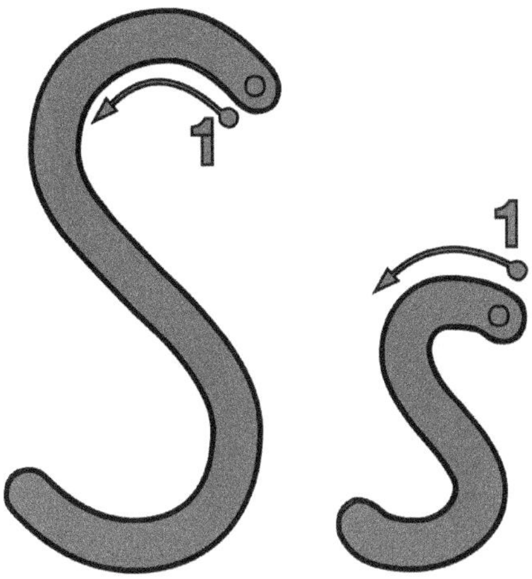

Ss

Seal

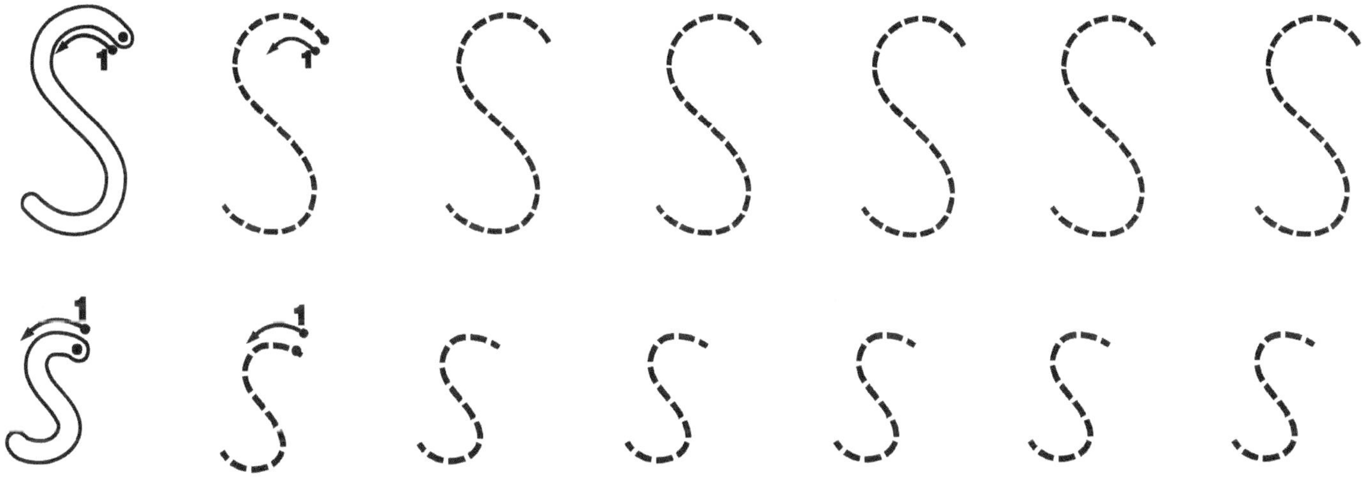

# Write the Letter T

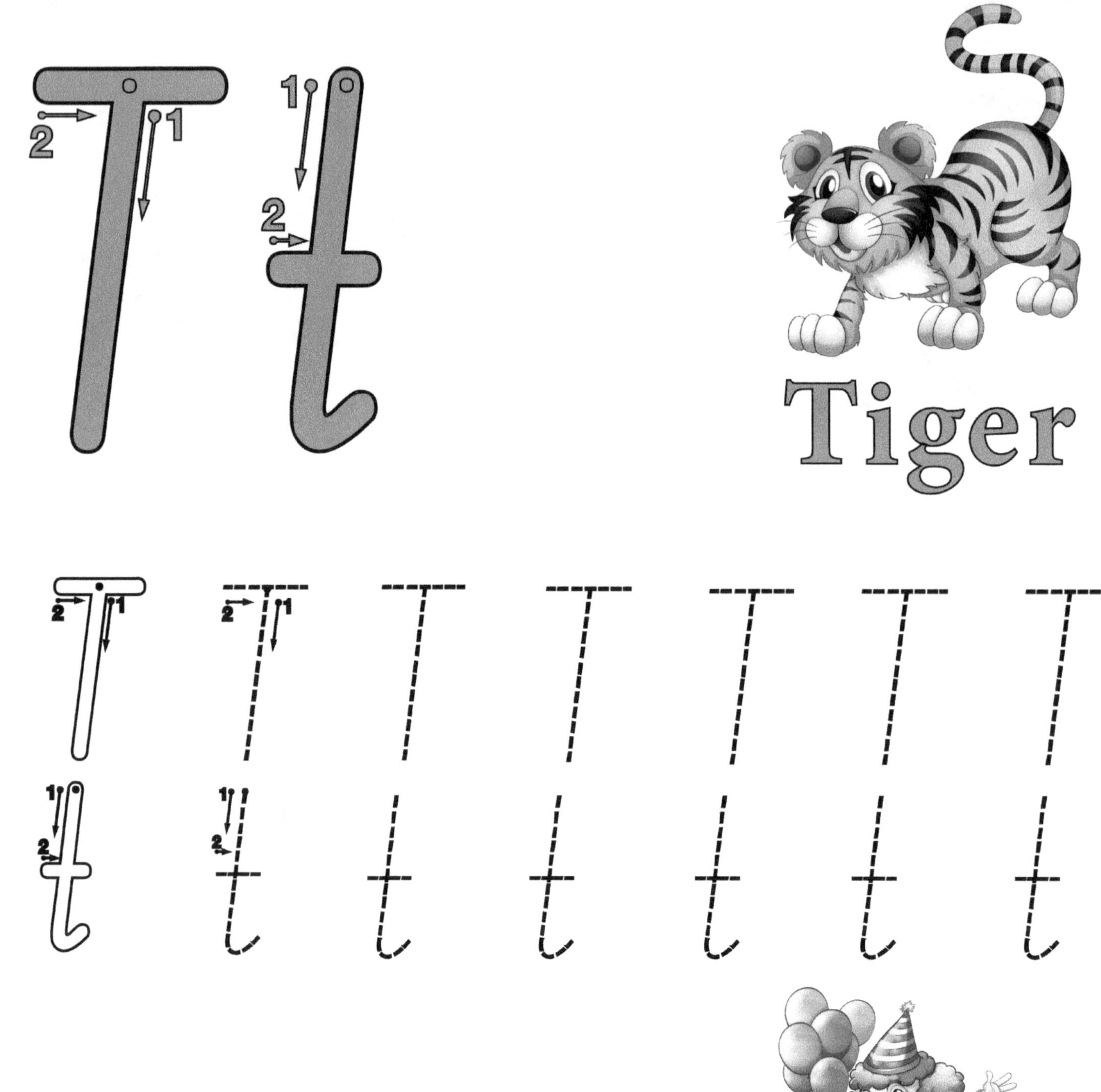

# Write the Letter U

Uu

Umbrella

U U U U U U U

u u u u u u u

# Write the Letter V

# Write the Letter W

# Write the Letter X

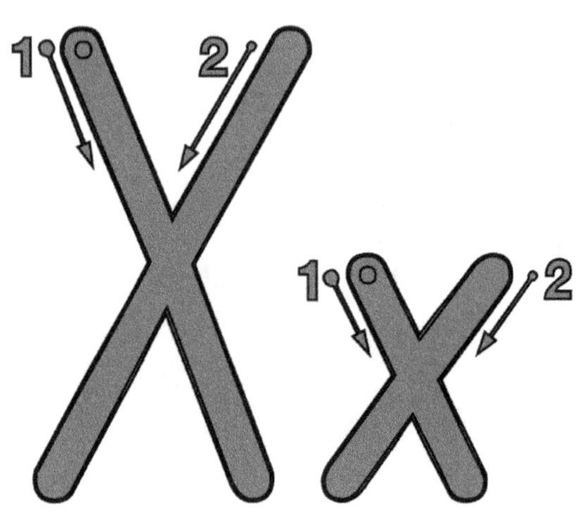

XERUS

# Write the Letter Y

# Write the Letter Z

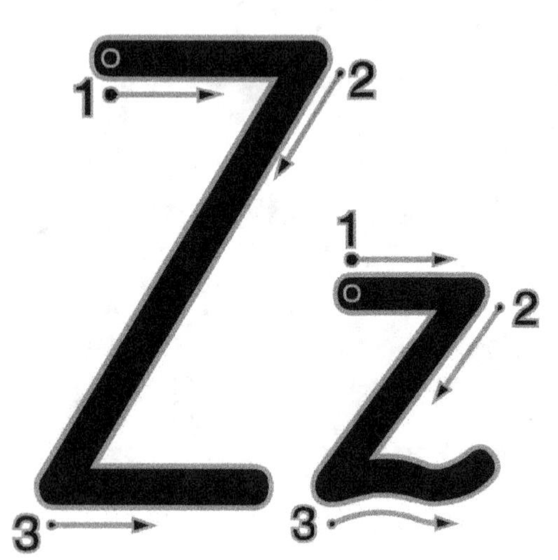

ZEBRA

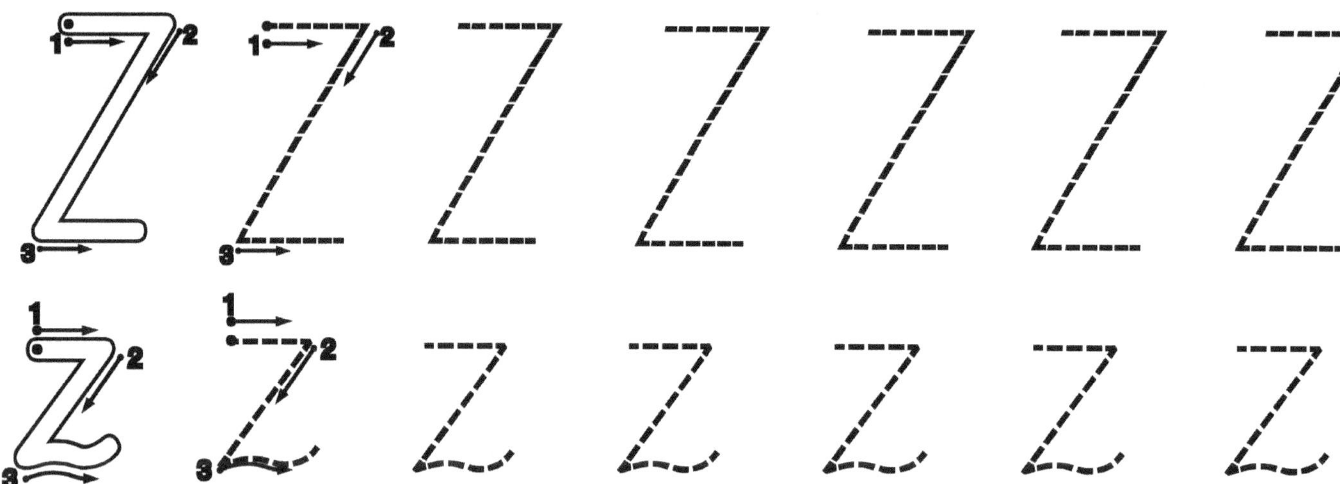

Science of Light and the Darkness of ignorance.

www.ingramcontent.com/pod-product-compliance
Lightning Source LLC
LaVergne TN
LVHW080057170826
845677LV00024B/1778
*9798714846502*